WAL

CALDI

HILLSIDE GUIDES - ACROSS NORTHERN ENGLAND

The Uplands of Britain - full colour hardback books
- **THE HIGH PEAKS OF ENGLAND & WALES**
- **YORKSHIRE DALES, MOORS & FELLS**

Long Distance Walks
- **COAST TO COAST WALK**
- **DALES WAY**
- **CUMBRIA WAY**
- **WESTMORLAND WAY**
- **FURNESS WAY**
- **LADY ANNE'S WAY**
- **BRONTE WAY**
- **PENDLE WAY**
- **NIDDERDALE WAY**
- **TRANS-PENNINE WAY**
- **CALDERDALE WAY**

Hillwalking - Lake District
- **LAKELAND FELLS - SOUTH**
- **LAKELAND FELLS - EAST**
- **LAKELAND FELLS - NORTH**
- **LAKELAND FELLS - WEST**

Circular Walks - Peak District
- **NORTHERN PEAK**
- **EASTERN PEAK**
- **CENTRAL PEAK**
- **SOUTHERN PEAK**
- **WESTERN PEAK**

Circular Walks - Yorkshire Dales
- **HOWGILL FELLS**
- **THREE PEAKS**
- **MALHAMDALE**
- **WHARFEDALE**
- **NIDDERDALE**
- **WENSLEYDALE**
- **SWALEDALE**
- **HARROGATE & WHARFE VALLEY**
- **RIPON & LOWER WENSLEYDALE**

Circular Walks - North East Yorkshire
- **NORTH YORK MOORS, SOUTHERN**
- **HOWARDIAN HILLS**

Circular Walks - South Pennines
- **BRONTE COUNTRY**
- **ILKLEY MOOR**
- **CALDERDALE**
- **SOUTHERN PENNINES**

Circular Walks - Lancashire/North West
- **BOWLAND**
- **PENDLE & THE RIBBLE**
- **WEST PENNINE MOORS**
- **ARNSIDE & SILVERDALE**
- **LUNESDALE**

Circular Walks - North Pennines
- **TEESDALE**
- **EDEN VALLEY**
- **ALSTON & ALLENDALE**

Short Scenic Walks
(full colour pocket-sized guidebooks to walks under 5 miles)
- **UPPER WHARFEDALE**
- **LOWER WHARFEDALE**
- **MALHAMDALE**
- **NIDDERDALE**
- **HARROGATE/KNARESBOROUGH**
- **AIRE VALLEY**
- **BOWLAND**
- **AMBLESIDE/LANGDALE**
- **BORROWDALE**

Send for a current catalogue and pricelist
or visit www.hillsidepublications.co.uk

WALKING COUNTRY

CALDERDALE WAY

Paul Hannon

HILLSIDE

HILLSIDE
PUBLICATIONS
20 Wheathead Crescent
Keighley
West Yorkshire
BD22 6LX

First published 2001
2nd impression (with amendments) 2009

© Paul Hannon 2001, 2009

ISBN 978 1 870141 71 0

Cover illustration: Waterfall in North Wood, Norwood Green
Back cover: Stone causey on Whirlaw;
Old Bridge Inn, Ripponden; Methodist chapel, Heptonstall
(Paul Hannon/Hillslides Picture Library)

Page One: Lumbutts Lane, Lumbutts
Page Three: Carving at Heptonstall

Printed in Great Britain by
Carnmor Print
95-97 London Road
Preston
Lancashire
PR1 4BA

CONTENTS

Hebble Hole Bridge, Colden Clough

INTRODUCTION

The Calderdale Way was devised in the early 1970s by a number of local civic trusts and groups who came together under the umbrella of the Calderdale Way Association, to create a walk showing off the innumerable attractions within the impending new local authority district of Calderdale. The interest of the Countryside Commission in helping develop 'Recreational Footpaths' in urban fringe areas brought grant aid that ensured the Way could become a practical reality, helping to fund path improvements, waymarking and a host of tasks behind the scenes.

Calderdale was established as a political entity on that shameful April Fool's Day 1974, which saw centuries of history 'abolished' in so many parts of the country. Calderdale is a compact geographical unit well defined for the most part by moorland watersheds with neighbouring valleys in both Yorkshire and Lancashire, and is the very heart and epitome of the South Pennines.

The River Calder has its beginnings on the soggy moors above Todmorden, but is quickly engulfed by urban scenes as it carves a deep course through the upper dale, past Hebden Bridge and Sowerby Bridge. By the time it reaches Brighouse the Calder's valley broadens considerably, the Pennine character vanishes, the pollution increases, and the river embarks on the remainder of its journey to meet the Aire at Castleford. It is perhaps convenient therefore that the local authority area to which the Way was dedicated should have its boundary below Brighouse, therefore guaranteeing the route a largely unblemished course through scenery of great variety and always much interest.

Interestingly enough, the river itself proves somewhat elusive on this walk. Other than being crossed at Todmorden, and again as a much greater watercourse just before completing the Way at West Vale, it is witnessed for just a brief spell from the canal towpath leaving Brighouse.

Calderdale's beauty is its unique blend of town and country: here the two are inextricably linked. The larger settlements squeeze sardine-like into the cramped valley floor, which is shared with river, canal, road and railway. Steep flanks rise in most cases to intervening ledges where older villages, predecessors of their bigger brothers below, almost shake hands across the deep divides. Higher still, rough pasture gives way to open moorland, where the mill chimney 2 miles away might as well be 200 miles distant.

Many features of the district's industrial past provide much of interest to the observant walker. The hills are laced with a centuries old network of trading routes used mainly by packhorses: many of these escaped 'improvement', and numerous sections of stone causeway have survived, laying virtually dormant in wait for today's foot traveller to bring them back to life, albeit for a new purpose. Hugging the valley bottom, in contrast, is the Rochdale Canal, which largely replaced the packhorse routes and whose towpath provides miles of leisurely, uninterrupted walking. In the lower dale, the Calder & Hebble Navigation provides a similar linear lung.

Tumbling to the floor of the upper dale at regular intervals are short lived but deep-cut and richly wooded little valleys known as cloughs, where some of the earliest mills were built in the most unlikely settings. Up on the tops one is never far from a reservoir, the earlier ones made to serve the canal, others to slake the ever-growing thirsts of the towns down the valley. This is definitive gritstone country, and sharing the higher ground with the reservoirs are clusters of boulders and crags, the weathered natural outcrops outshining the countless sites of former quarries. Mainly small-scale operations known as 'delphs', they provided material for the hoary drystone walls, reservoirs and buildings throughout the dale.

The administrative centre of Calderdale is Halifax, a lively town that offers much to the visitor. Shopping and culture are combined at the famous Piece Hall: if you see nothing else, this is a must. Built in the 18th century as a merchants' cloth hall, it was lovingly restored in the 1970s and its galleries now feature a wealth of fascinating shops. Markets are held in the centre, and weekend attractions regularly include brass bands amongst the entertainment. Also in Halifax are an industrial museum, a unique children's 'hands on' museum, Shibden Hall with its folk museum, and the Bankfield Museum.

The waymarking and condition of paths is very good overall, an indication of the local authority's highly commendable valuation of its outstanding path network. A feature of the Way is the vast number of 'Link Paths' connecting the main route with the valley. These are so numerous that they receive no special mention in the text, though they cannot be missed on the ground. There are of course any number of other linking routes available by a simple glance at the 1:25,000 scale map.

The Calderdale Way is a splendid example of what can be achieved in what was once deemed an 'unfashionable' walking area, and its subsequent popularity is a fitting tribute to the work of those involved in its creation.

Getting around
The Way is ideally placed for walking in separate day sections, with many West Yorkshire and Lancashire conurbations close to hand. There are ample bus services at numerous points along the way, many in the most unlikely locations. Either way, the valley floor and/or main roads are never very distant from any part of the walk. Convenient rail stations are found at Todmorden, Hebden Bridge, Mytholmroyd, Sowerby Bridge, Halifax and Brighouse.

Using the guide
The main section of the guide is a detailed description of the route and its associated features. Divided into four manageable sections, each offers a steady ramble with good transport links. A compromise for very strong walkers would be to spend a strenuous weekend over it, but even then, many features of interest would be missed in the desire to tick the miles off.

Each of the four stages is self-contained, with the essential information being followed by a simple map and a concise route description. Dovetailed in between are notes of features along the way, and interspersed are illustrations which capture the flavour of the walk and document many items of interest. Essential route description has been highlighted in bold, in order to make it easily accessible in amongst the other snippets of information. The sketch maps serve only to identify the location of the route, and whilst the description should be sufficient to guide one around, an Ordnance Survey map is strongly recommended.

The entire route is covered by only two maps at the 1:25,000 scale. They are indispensible companions to the guidebook, as both have the route highlighted:

●Explorer OL21 - *South Pennines*
●Explorer 288 - *Bradford & Huddersfield*

Additionally, at the 1:50,000 scale (particularly useful for planning purposes) the route is covered by:

●Landranger 103 - *Blackburn & Burnley*
●Landranger 104 - *Leeds, Bradford & Harrogate*
●Landranger 110 - *Sheffield & Huddersfield*
(tiny section of the latter only, at Ripponden)

HEBDEN BRIDGE

Though not on the route, this self-proclaimed 'South Pennine Centre' is undeniably the focal point for the Calderdale Way. It is to here that most of the modern tourists make, partly for its position at the foot of the famous Hebden Dale (universally Hardcastle Crags), but also for its own attractions. Its houses climb alarmingly up the steep hillsides above the meeting of the valleys, while the lively centre includes a good selection of pubs, cafes, collectors' shops, craft shops and an invaluable information centre.

The town featured prominently on the old trans-Pennine packhorse route from Burnley to Halifax, and the pack bridge over Hebden Water dates back to the 16th century. Hebden Bridge's development owed much to the harnessing of its fast flowing streams to power the flourishing textile mills, while the Rochdale Canal and its successor the railway forged parallel routes through the valley. Today, canal cruises operate from the small marina, and gentle but absorbing strolls can be enjoyed along the towpath.

Hebden Bridge is best accessed from the Way where it meets Hebden Water just short of Hardcastle Crags: a waymarked route sets off downstream (part of the 'Haworth to Hebden Bridge Walk').

Hebden Bridge

SOME USEFUL FACILITIES

A general guide only

	Youth Hostel	Accommodation	Bus service	Rail station	Pub	Shop	WC	Cafe
West Vale		•			•	•	•	•
Greetland		•	•		•	•		
Norland		•	•		•		•	
Ripponden		•	•		•	•	•	•
Soyland		•						
Mill Bank		•			•			
Cragg Vale		•	•		•		•	
Mankinholes	•	•	•					
Lumbutts		•			•			
Todmorden		•	•	•	•	•	•	•
Blackshaw Head		•	•					
Colden		•			•	•		
Heptonstall		•	•		•	•	•	
Midgehole		•					•	•
Hebden Bridge		•	•	•	•	•	•	•
Pecket Well		•	•		•			
Old Town		•	•		•			
Mytholmroyd		•	•	•	•	•	•	•
Midgley		•	•					
Luddenden		•			•		•	
Jerusalem/Booth		•					•	
Wainstalls		•			•			
Upper Brockholes		•	•		•			
Bradshaw		•			•			
Holdsworth		•	•		•			
Catherine Slack		•						
Stone Chair		•	•		•	•		
Shelf		•	•		•	•	•	
Norwood Green		•			•			
Bailiff Bridge		•			•	•	•	
Brighouse		•	•	•	•	•	•	•
Southowram		•			•	•		

SOME USEFUL ADDRESSES

The Ramblers
2nd Floor, Camelford House, 87-89 Albert Embankment,
London SE1 7BR
Tel. 020-7339 8500

Calderdale Countryside and Forestry Unit
Wesley Court, Crossley Street, Halifax HX1 1UJ
Tel. 01422-393214

Tourist Information

Visitor Centre & Art Gallery, Piece Hall **Halifax** HX1 1RE
Tel. 01422-368725

Visitor & Canal Centre, Butlers Wharf, New Road
Hebden Bridge HX7 8AF
Tel. 01422-843831

15 Burnley Road **Todmorden** OL14 7BU
Tel. 01706-818181

South Pennine Packhorse Trails Trust
The Barn, Mankinholes, Todmorden OL14 6HR
Tel. 01706-815598

Pennine Heritage
The Birchcliffe Centre, Hebden Bridge HX7 8DG
Tel. 01422-844450
(an environmental, charitable trust dedicated to maintaining the
unique heritage of the South Pennine area)

Metro (West Yorkshire buses and trains)
Wellington House, 40-50 Wellington Street, Leeds LS1 2DE
Tel. 0113-245 7676

National Rail Enquiry Line
Tel. 08457-484950

STAGE 1

WEST VALE *to* MANKINHOLES

Distance: 13½ miles/21½km

Map:
1:50,000
Landranger 103 - Blackburn & Burnley
Landranger 104 - Leeds, Bradford & Harrogate
Landranger 110 - Sheffield & Huddersfield
1:25,000
Outdoor Leisure 21 - South Pennines

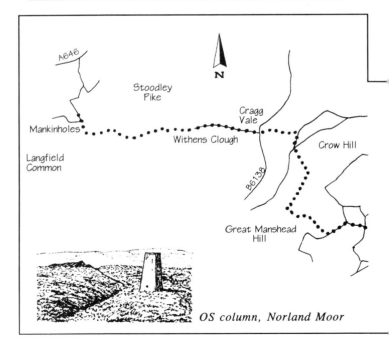

OS column, Norland Moor

➧ **The Calderdale Way begins and ends at Clay House, just off the B6113 Rochdale Road at West Vale crossroads.** Clay House is a most impressive yeoman clothier's house with a fine facade of mullioned and transomed windows. Dating from the 17th century, it is managed by the local authority. Alongside is an aisled barn with a magnificent low slung roof (illustrated on page 45). It was restored in 1986 and converted into private dwellings. Note that the opening half-mile of the Way has changed from its original route, opting for a slightly more circuitous course for earlier access to North Dean Wood.

Begin by passing between the house and the old barn, and up a small grassy area to a broad track behind a wall gap on the edge of woodland. Turn right on this just a few yards, then bear left on a waymarked path. Through a bridle-gate it enters deeper woodland, and sets off along the course of an old railway. This short branch line to Stainland opened in 1875, and closed in the 1950s. **After a short way a waymarked path rises left through the wood, through a wall-gap onto another path. Keep right on this broad path, rising slightly to meet a level embanked path from the left. Continue to the right, looking down on the noise and industry of the valley floor. Running on to a fork, take the left branch for a splendid steady rise through North Dean Wood, with clusters of tumbled boulders above.**

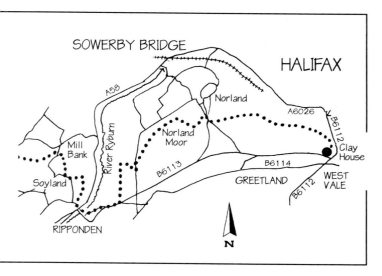

At the top a path is joined and followed right for a considerable time, with very steep woods below and fields to the left. This grand stride eventually emerges onto a rough road. Just half a minute to the right, a path bears off left to resume a woodtop ramble, initially gently uphill. Snatched views to the valley feature Copley Viaduct, with a low arched rail bridge in front of it.

A stile takes us out of the wood, but the direction is unchanged as we tramp the edge of a massive pasture, sadly not the Greetland Moor anticipated from the map. During a faint rise the path broadens into a track, while the adjacent woodland gives way to heather moorland; Norland Moor is in view ahead. The track ultimately leads to Turbury Lane. Go right the few yards to Clough Moor Bridge, merging with Norland Road en route. Set into the bridge is a boundary stone, marked *Division of Norland and Elland.* **Across it, bear left on a broad path onto Norland Moor. This quickly rises to a wall corner under a pylon. Turn left on the wallside path along the edge of the heathery moor.**

Norland Moor is an island-like heather tract perching high above Sowerby Bridge and the Ryburn Valley. Publicly owned since 1932, it bears the much healed scars of extensive small-scale quarrying, notably along the western escarpment. Immediately north of the moor the sprawl of Halifax dominates, with the nearby Wainhouse Tower (a famous landmark built in the 1870s to serve a dyeworks) completely dwarfing the many mill chimneys and church spires. Also north of the moor is Norland 'Town', an isolated hilltop settlement boasting some rather splendid clothiers' houses of centuries past. It provides a rapid descent link into Sowerby Bridge.

At a waymark and scrappy cairn turn sharp right, a broad path rising ever gently over the heart of the moor, over a path crossroads to reach a main path in front of a covered reservoir. Ahead are grand views over the Ryburn Valley to Crow Hill and Manshead Hill, while southwards the expanse of Norland Moor appears greater than it really is. **Turn left along the main path, a grand tramp above the more extensive quarries of Turgate Delph.** Just below on the roadside is the *Moorcock Inn*, to which a broad quarrymans' track runs down for emergency refreshment.

Ahead is an Ordnance Survey column at 931ft/284m, to which a branch path duly turns off. Though appearing to be so, this is not quite the loftiest point, although the ominous sounding Gallows Pole Hill, a third of a mile to the south, still doesn't earn a 1000 foot contour. **A return path rejoins the main route just a little further, conveniently alongside the Ladstone Rock.** This gritstone outcrop is a distinctive landmark, bearing a 'psalm-plaque' of which several are scattered around the district. This is a good place to halt and take in the sweeping view across the deep gulf of the Ryburn Valley to Crow Hill, Great Manshead Hill, Rishworth Moor and Blackstone Edge, with the M62 motorway further south across Saddleworth Moor.

The Ladstone Rock

Resuming along the edge, Ripponden at once appears in the valley below. The path soon drops towards the road, Butterworth End Lane, though a branch forges on a little further to the moor corner. Advance along the footway just as far as the *New Rock Inn*, then double back right on an access road, Highlee Lane. Remain on this as it drops down, continually improving. Narrowing into a footway, it steepens and becomes a little untidy, whereupon take a stile on the left and cross the field bottom to an enclosed track.

The track runs on past a house at Moor Bottom and continues as its level drive, Moor Bottom Road, all the way along to Elland Road (B6113) at Ripponden Bank Top. This spell enjoys views beyond Ripponden to Rishworth Moor. **Turn down the road to the *Fleece*. Just below the pub the old road (Ripponden Old Bank) bears right and runs a direct, steeper traffic-free course down into Ripponden, with the church spire directly below. The village is entered at an attractive corner at Bridge End.**

Ripponden is a busy village, its old centre being a conservation area. St. Bartholomew's church spire reaches to the heavens, while a restored packhorse bridge forges a good partnership with the white-walled and equally historic *Old Bridge Inn*. Beneath the bridge flows the river Ryburn. The railway arrived from Sowerby Bridge in 1881 and closed in 1958: sections have been put to good use as permissive paths. **Go straight on from the church over the packhorse bridge to the incognito *Old Bridge Inn*, and then continue up Priest Lane onto the A58.**

At Ripponaen

Straight over the main road, head up the steep Royd Lane. As it narrows, turn right on a short enclosed way, and as the path splits take the stile on the left into a field. A causeyed path runs across two fields, then a short way through the next before becoming enclosed. It runs on to the short terrace at Birks. At the end, take the stile/gate in front and ascend a gently rising walled way, as far as a sharp bend. From the stile in front, advance along the wallside to join an enclosed rough road at the far end. Turn up this (Cow Lane) to enter Soyland Town, emerging opposite some attractive mullioned windows. Soyland is a tiny hilltop community that saw far busier times when the cottage weaving industry was in its heyday.

Go right along the street to the drive of Making Place Farm with its big barn on the left. Here take a flagged path on the right, down a fieldside to join a drive. Oddly, the short length of path is shown as neither Calderdale Way nor even right of way on the map. Continue down this, but well before the house take a stile on the left. Head away with a wall which descends the fieldsides. The side valley of Severhills Clough appears ahead, with the settlement of Mill Bank in front. Our way becomes enclosed to ultimately descend steps onto a track (Clapgate Lane), with a road just down to the left. Turn right down the road (Foxen Lane) to the bridge at Mill Bank. The heart of this unassuming backwater is up the hill in front, where a seemingly haphazard cluster of houses climb above each other.

Without crossing, turn left up an inviting streamside track, keeping straight on into woodland beyond the house its serves. A grand path slants up through some woodland not shown on the map, emerging at the top onto a surfaced drive to the isolated house at Wood End. Turn up this hairpin and follow the access road (Gough Lane) up onto Lighthazles Road at Eccles Parlour. Head up the road almost opposite, becoming Cross Dikes Road, a traffic-free climb to a T-junction. Go left here (Ash Hall Lane), ignoring an early bridleway doubling back right, and keep on to a walled access track on the right. This climbs gently to a fork. The right branch goes to Flints Hall, while Manshead Hill appears over to the left.

Take neither branch, but from the stile in front, the path runs along the southern embankment of the former Flints Reservoir. At the end it advances across the moor to a wall corner, behind which a track is joined. This runs the same course along to a prominent ruin at Slate Delfs Hill. This curious red-brick structure is the remains of a decoy site, intended to confuse German bombers during the Second World War. Just behind it is a crossroads of tracks. Turn right, enjoying a lengthy high altitude stride on the inviting green track of Water

Stalls Road. The Ordnance Survey column on Crow Hill is prominent ahead, with Wainhouse Tower, Halifax and Norland Moor seen beyond.

Though it soon leaves the moor, the largely enclosed way runs grandly on. Ovenden Moor windfarm is seen ahead to the left of Crow Hill, while over to the left is the unmistakeable Stoodley Pike monument. **The grassy way fades at a gate onto open grassy land at the end. Turn left on the wallside, the track re-forming to slant down rough moorland, and then down past Catherine House and out on the drive onto a road junction.** Catherine House is notable for its remarkable early 19th century chimney, put to various uses down the years.

Cross straight over and along Coppy Nook Lane, just as far as High Lane, an access road down to the left. Ahead, the Withens Clough stage of the Way is well seen climbing to the grassy dam and moorland across Cragg Vale. **The road descends steeply, largely surfaced at first, to a fork. Bear right along here to a gate, and through it the track winds down to a renovated house. To its left a grassy little path runs down a heathery wallside to a little gate in a stile, then largely flagged down a steep colourful bank. At the bottom a stile sends the path contouring left, then angling down, still flagged, to join a steeply ascending walled way. Turn down this to a drive, then down the drive onto Cragg Road in Cragg Vale at Four Gate End.**

Go right a few yards then double back down the steep Church Bank, with the church below and the pub just behind. Cragg Vale's claim to infamy is as the home of the Yorkshire Coiners. It is the most romantically recalled (though far from only) site of 18th century counterfeiting: this practice involved clipping gold from guineas to make additional, inferior coins. At the end of Stage 2 we can see the grave of 'King' David Hartley, a ringleader who was hanged for his crimes. The sombre church of St. John the Baptist in the Wilderness dates from 1839, while the adjacent *Hinchliffe Arms* displays some coiners memorabilia.

The Te Deum Stone,
Withens Gate

Advance straight along the road, ignoring any branches. An attractive lodge is passed, while a circular chimney stands forlorn over to the left. **A steady haul leads up Withens Clough to the road-end at a car park. Keep straight on the firm access road to the embankment of Withens Clough Reservoir, and on its side past a lone house.** The reservoir was completed in 1894 for Morley Corporation: while moorland occupies the opposite bank, its legacy on our side is unkempt pastures and a score of crumbling walls.

Remain on the rough road until the second signed path on the right. A grassy track ascends to a wall corner, then keep on to the wall junction just behind. Also a junction of ways, turn left through a stile and follow a superb causeyed path along the wallside for some time. Towards the end the path takes to the other side, then quickly to the wall-end and off along open moor. More flagging is uncovered before joining a broader path. Remain on this to arrive at a wall, where turn sharp right and ascend with the wall to gain the moor top at Withens Gate. In front of the stile stands the squat Te Deum Stone. Its Latin inscription means *We praise thee O Lord!*, and being on the summit of the Mankinholes-Withens track is likely to have been used for resting coffins.

The Long Stoop

Through the gate the broad green path is accompanied by stone marker posts. The upper dale opens out in grand style, revealing an entirely new landscape. **More flags materialise to lead to a major crossroads of moorland ways.** This is overseen by the Long Stoop, an old guidepost of monumental stature. Here the modern foot traveller's highway, the celebrated Pennine Way, meets a centuries old packhorse route known (like several others) as the Long Causeway. This is the first of two meetings with the PW, and very much a place to sit and take stock.

Along to the right rises the monument on Stoodley Pike, and a well-worn path tempts an easy, level detour. The monument was erected in 1815 to celebrate peace after victory over Napoleon, but later collapsed and was replaced in 1856. It stands a mighty 120ft above the 1300ft moortop, and is the upper valley's most famous landmark. A dark spiral staircase climbs 39 steps to a viewing balcony:

the 360° degree panorama features moorland skylines in almost every direction. Todmorden sits in the valley ahead, with Coal Clough windfarm behind. Immediately below us, Mankinholes and Lumbutts occupy the shelf that hides so much of the valley bottom.

Stoodley Pike from the Pennine Way near Withens Gate

Resuming straight ahead, arguably the finest of Calderdale's old causeys awaits. This splendidly preserved section of flags can be seen leading all the way down towards Mankinholes. Faithfully tread this remarkable path as it slants down to a wall corner then down its side to the bottom corner of the moor. While the direct course of the causey to Lumbutts is straight ahead, the Way takes a stile/gate on the right and along an enclosed track to Mankinholes. Mankinholes is an old handloom weaving settlement largely by-passed by the 20th century. The great water troughs are a sign of its importance in packhorse days. Today, most visitors are youth hostellers breaking their Pennine Way journey in the shadow of Stoodley Pike.

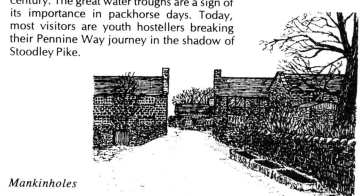

Mankinholes

STAGE 2

MANKINHOLES *to* HEPTONSTALL

Distance: 11½ miles/18½km

Map:
1:50,000
Landranger 103 - Blackburn & Burnley
1:25,000
Outdoor Leisure 21 - South Pennines

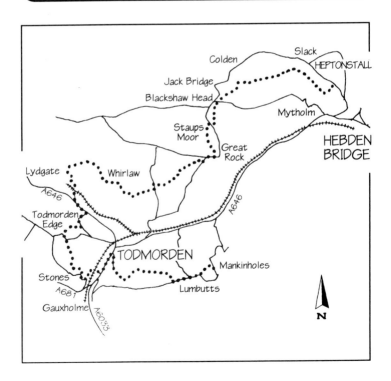

➡️ **Advance through the hamlet of Mankinholes to the last buildings, and on a little further to a house that was originally a Wesleyan Methodist Sunday School.** This is the site of Mankinholes Methodist Church, built 1814, enlarged 1870 rebuilt 1911, closed 1979, demolished 1981. **Opposite the burial ground, turn left down the paved Lumbutts Lane to the sprawling *Top Brink Inn* at Lumbutts.** At the foot of the lane is a milestone inscribed *Halifax* and *Heptonstall*.

Lumbutts is an attractive settlement which nestles in a hollow below Mankinholes. It is entirely dominated by a former water wheel tower that served a cotton mill that stood here. This immense structure contained three vertically arranged wheels, each fed from above as well as independently. Immediately above the tower is Lee Dam, one of three tree-lined dams hovering above the hamlet, and the scene of an annual New Year 'dip' for the hardiest of souls.

Water wheel tower, Lumbutts

In front, a short setted footway drops down onto the road, with the water wheel tower alongside. Head away along the road for a steady half-mile rise. Roadside houses en route feature a sundial of 1864 and a 400 year old datestone. **Turn off at a drive on the right at Croft Gate. Head along this, passing between two houses to a gate in front, and a walled grassy way heads away. Before the corner take a stile on the left, and head away along the pathless wallside. From a stile at the end resume on the other side of the wall to a brow. Maintain this course down and through two field centres to Higher Longfield Farm.** From these fields Todmorden re-appears. Directly ahead on the facing slope is Dobroyd Castle, further along our route. **Entering the yard by a stile onto the drive, bear round to the left and take a stile in front of cottages. A few uncovered flags cross a paddock to an equestrian centre. Advance straight on past myriad stables and horses, and out along the drive at the end. Remain on it as it swings left and along to a surfaced road end. Here turn right, a rough walled track passing beneath a grassy embankment and revealing a part-flagged centre as it swings downhill.**

The way becomes surfaced as Shoebroad Lane at some cottages, and drops down into Todmorden past the old Unitarian Church. Dating from 1869, it boasts a very prominent spire and was built by the then influential Fielden family. These final stages enjoy views of town centre features such as the Town Hall and the railway viaduct. **Continue down this road to emerge via Honey Hole Road at Fielden Square by the *Golden Lion*. The town centre is one minute to the right.**

On first impressions Hebden Bridge's partner Todmorden may have less obvious charm, but it quickly proves to be a smashing place to explore and boasts numerous outstanding buildings. Pride of place goes to the Town Hall. Designed by Fielden's architect John Gibson in 1875, it features a group of marble figures on a pediment above tall columns. Tucked away up a side street is Todmorden Old Hall, built in 1603 by the Ratcliffes. With a stunning frontage of gables and mullioned and transomed windows, it is currently a restaurant. St. Mary's parish church is centrally sited but also tucked away.

The Old Hall, Todmorden

Unlike its Calderdale counterparts which thrived on the woollen industry, Todmorden and its mills were geared to the Lancashire cotton industry. Indeed, until a century ago Todmorden was quite literally on the border. Of the three roads heading out, two still aim for the red rose towns of Rochdale and Burnley, both more accessible than Todmorden's Yorkshire masters: a hint of divided loyalties clearly remains hereabouts!

Head left along Rochdale Road (A6033) as far as Morrisons supermarket, then turn along the rough Dobroyd Road on the right. This bridges the Rochdale Canal and rises to the railway line. The Rochdale Canal was completed in 1804, running 33 miles between Manchester and the Calder & Hebble Navigation at Sowerby Bridge. Sadly its heyday was but a brief one, and the demise began in 1841 when the Lancashire & Yorkshire Railway was completed. Thus the canals, whose far greater efficiency had replaced packhorses, were themselves quickly ousted by the vastly improved service the railways offered. By 1922 commercial traffic had virtually ceased.

Across the canal, take the main rough road rising left, climbing through the outer grounds of Dobroyd Castle and up through woodland with increasing views up the valley. Ultimately it joins the surfaced Stones Road alongside a lodge. The drive leads to Dobroyd Castle, built in the 1860s for the influential Fielden family, mill owners and local benefactors. John Fielden, MP for Oldham, is best known. He was instrumental in the passing of the 10 Hour Act in 1847, which meant women and children were saved from working more than 10 hours per day! The gaunt house spent a dozen years as a Buddhist retreat until 2007: it is now a children's activity centre.

Continue straight up Stones Road. Further improved views up the valley are equalled by those back down the dale, where Stoodley Pike enjoys its usual moor-edge setting. **Up through a hairpin the road runs beneath former Lob Quarry and above Pex House, becoming rougher surfaced with views down over Dobroyd Castle. Advance along, swinging left to rise to an old house at Stones. Alongside it turn right along an access track.** To the right is an architecturally intriguing former coach house, now two dwellings.

Passing one house to a stile behind, we leave the now green way as our old way swings up the open field, an obvious sunken course to the wall at the top. Advance along this grand embanked stride through two gateways and out via a stile onto a narrow road. This last section is arguably upper Calderdale's finest viewpoint. **Bear left on here for only a minute, then drop right, down a rough road to a cluster of buildings at Todmorden Edge. When it turns left, take**

a walled green way on the right before the Old Golf House, descending pleasantly into a field. We are still savouring massive views across the narrowing upper valley, with the knoll of Whirlaw prominent, as well as the Bride Stones, Hawks Stones, the Long Causeway and Coal Clough windfarm.

At the bottom a gate admits to the top of Buckley Wood. The path traverses right along the wood top before slanting down the steep beechwood onto Ewood Lane above Centre Vale Park. The park was bought from the Fielden family in 1910 for the benefit of the local population, and it features a fine statue of the previously mentioned John Fielden. Also here are a War Memorial garden, aviary and aquarium, and enough open space for every family in town. **Double back down the road, past a tearoom and out past a new sports centre and Todmorden High School onto the main road.** The infant Calder is crossed here. Across the road, the *Hare & Hounds* pub is no longer dwarfed by the massive, red-brick Mons Mill, a major landmark until its demolition in 2000.

Go left for a few minutes towards Lydgate, then bear right on Stoney Royd Lane. Past urban housing a drive runs on to The Glen: keep right, on the rough road to pass under an immense railway arch. A drive then rises to Stannally Farm, doubling back up behind it and spiralling steeply through woods. Climbing alongside a deep wooded clough, it emerges at the top onto the foot of the open country of Stannally Stones. Prominent over to the left are Orchan Rocks.

Bear right on the access track slanting up to the very isolated Rake Hey Farm. Pass along its rear and an old walled footway climbs to join the contouring course of Stony Lane. This splendid track is an old packhorse route with which we are to become well acquainted. The views are very typical Calderdale: windfarm, moors, farms, rocks, and the Cliviger and Walsden gorges. For a time the populated valley floor, with its railway line and busy road, is entirely hidden by the slopes beneath us.

At Whirlaw _____

Turn right along the splendid track, soon emerging to cross a pasture on flags to reach Whirlaw Common. Take the main path bearing right, a superb flagged way curving beneath Whirlaw Stones. Whirlaw Stones form a well defined edge high above our stone causeway, its gritstone boulders interlaced with patches of heather. **At the**

end the path becomes enclosed to run on above the farm at West Whirlaw, and on above East Whirlaw to join a farm road. Turn right down this, soon entering a wooded clough. On easing out it swings round to a crossroads of such ways, with a lone house to the left. Go straight across, but within a few yards take a stile on the left.

Climb the field to another stile then head away with the wall. From the gateway at the top, rise gently and faintly across a couple of reedy pastures to a stile onto Todmorden golf course. Keep to the wallside path on the left to run along to a stile onto a road, Hey Head Lane. Climb left 100 yards to West Hey Head Farm then turn right along a short-lived farm drive.

Pass the rear of the buildings at East Hey Head to a stile, then across a couple of fields to meet a sunken, heathery banked way. Cross straight over onto the heathery hummocks of Law Hill. A common sight in these parts is the old 'delph', scene of small-scale quarrying in times past. Most of this stage enjoys excellent views to Stoodley Pike rising ever prominently across the valley. For the most part there is virtually no evidence that we are in industrial Calderdale, for the shelves of lush, walled pastures that characterise this part of the dale entirely hide the deep valley bottom. **Over Law Hill, the Way drops quickly down to another green walled footway. Resume straight across, then along a field edge towards a house.**

Ignoring a stile into buildings, keep left and on to the far corner, crossing an overgrown sunken way. From here the path continues across a pasture and crosses a tiny clough. While its original course rises to the house at Higher Birks, the path is sent up to the left to pass above the house. At the other side a sunken pathway slants up between long abandoned walls to a wall: rise left on a track then turn right on a better, short-lived one. A path takes over, becoming more enclosed as it runs a level course out to an ascending road.

Go left the few yards to a junction, then right to the prominent and aptly named Great Rock. The obligatory carved initials and professions of undying love are joined by the official vandalism of a painted Calderdale Way stencil, more recently chiselled off but then restored! Scramble to the top and enjoy the view.

Great Rock

Leave the road by an enclosed grassy track to the left of the rock to a corner of Staups Moor. There are views ahead to Heptonstall and to Hebden Bridge on the valley floor. **The path stays with the right-hand wall to drop down to a ladder-stile off the moor. A faint path drops slightly right down a rough pasture onto the road at Hippins Bridge. Across, turn right on a short drive to Hippins.** This lovely old house of dark millstone grit boasts mullioned windows and a 1650s initialled datestone.

Immediately after the house turn left up past a large old barn to a stile behind, and a path climbs the fields to Apple Tree Farm. Cross straight over the drive and up a flagged path, this one intriguing in that it entirely bridges a streamlet all the way up to the house above. Passing this, a part flagged way rises up the next field, then a firm flagged one runs up to a yard. Go left up the short driveway onto the road at Blackshaw Head.

Just a couple of yards right, a stile opposite sends a path half-right across two flagged fields. On the brow the upper Colden Valley is revealed. Bear right down the next field to a crumbled corner, and maintain this generally obvious course down several fields to meet an enclosed walled pathway, Bow Lane. Descend this to a house at Shawbottom and then down a few yards further onto the access road. Note that the *New Delight* pub is just two minutes along to the left at Jack Bridge. **Turning right, ignore the road's crossing of the clough, and remain on a broad bridle-track for a short while. When a path drops left follow it down the heathery and stony bank to the waiting Hebble Hole Bridge.** This characterful, ancient footbridge consists of four great stone slabs in tandem in a charming location (illustrated on page 5). Here the Pennine and Calderdale Ways have the second of their two meetings.

Across, turn right on a flagged way downstream, quickly rising to a fork. Leaving the Pennine Way, go right on a splendid flagged panniermans' way above the beck. On entering Foster Wood, almost at once a fork sends our way left to a stile out of the trees, and the causey runs on through several fields above the wood. An enclosed flagless section leads on to meet a rising path. Bear left up this to join an access track. Turn right on this the short way to a house, passing along the rear to see another good flagged section head away. This runs to a path junction marked by a seat.

Take the way slanting gently right ahead, down and then on past a spring to meet a narrow ascending road, Green Lane. The house at Lumb Bank, just below, was the home of the Poet Laureate of recent times, Ted Hughes. **Rise up this until a gateway admits into**

the top of Eaves Wood on the right. A grand path clambers through boulders and along the wood top to emerge into open surrounds. This section reveals dramatic views from airy gritstone outcrops down steep heather and bilberry slopes into Colden Clough. Particularly grand is Stoodley Pike's monument high above the valley floor.

The Calder Valley from Eaves Wood, looking to Stoodley Pike

The path remains with the left-hand wall until an enclosed path strikes reluctantly off to the left. The tower of Heptonstall church beckons less since the appearance of modern housing that is visible, not surprisingly, from much of upper Calderdale. To finish simply keep straight on to emerge beneath the church. Past here there are a couple of minor branches that will lead back onto the main street. To incorporate the old church en route, jink left up under an archway beyond the church, to emerge alongside the old church and also the museum. This path emerges onto the main street next to the Cloth Hall opposite the *Cross Inn.*

Heptonstall is a fascinating village that well merits an hour's leisurely exploration. Steeped in history, it was of greater importance than Hebden Bridge until the arrival of the Industrial Revolution. Happily its exposed position 850 feet up and defended on three sides by precipitous slopes has created a time warp in which its weather-beaten stone cottages revel. Focal point is the churchyard which separates the imposing parish church of 1854 from the shell of the old church of St. Thomas a'Becket, partly dating from the 13th century. The notorious coiner 'King' David Hartley was buried here in 1770, and his grave can be found between the two churches. Alongside is the former grammar school of 1772 (founded 1642, closed 1889), now operating as a museum. Seek out also the old dungeon (1824), Chantry House and the 16th century Cloth Hall, the oldest town cloth hall in Yorkshire. Just up the street is a second pub, the *White Lion*.

STAGE 3

HEPTONSTALL *to* CATHERINE SLACK

Distance: 11½ miles/18½km

Map:
1:50,000
Landranger 103 - Blackburn & Burnley
Landranger 104 - Leeds, Bradford & Harrogate
1:25,000
Outdoor Leisure 21 - South Pennines

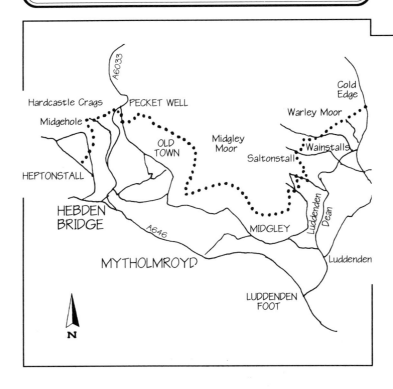

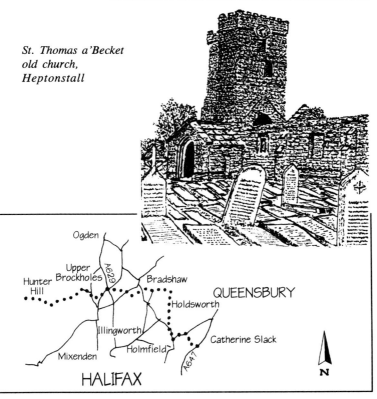

St. Thomas a'Becket old church, Heptonstall

➡️   Alongside the *Cross Inn* turn along Northgate. Part way on, note the carved figures above a door on the left. **Unmistakeable on the right is the splendid octagonal Wesleyan chapel of 1764. After the chapel the Way is signed down to the right, with the woods of Hardcastle Crags ahead. An enclosed path becomes a rougher drive to descend onto a road by an old milepost. Cross over and down through holly-rich woods, on a good path down over a drive to the sizeable Hebden Water.** A link path runs from here to Hebden Bridge. **The beck is followed upstream to New Bridge, by way of Midgehole Working Men's Club (known as the *Blue Pig*). Cross the bridge and up past Newbridge Hall to the main car park for Hardcastle Crags.**

A WALK TO HARDCASTLE CRAGS & CRIMSWORTH DEAN

5½ miles/9km from the National Trust car park at Midgehole

From the car park head up the drive a few yards to just past the solitary lodge, then fork left on a path descending to Hebden Water. A wide beckside path then leads upstream for almost a mile and a half to Gibson Mill, rarely straying far from the bank. Gibson Mill was founded in 1800 as an early water-powered cotton mill. It ceased to operate in the 1890s, becoming a curiously-sited dance hall and even a roller-skating rink during the mid-20th century. With related features including a row of workers cottages, the building is an imposing sight in its wooded environs. Round the back are a surviving millpond and cut.

Stepping stones, Gibson Mill

At Gibson Mill the driveway is rejoined to climb above the beck, and levels out alongside the steep rise of Hardcastle Crags. These modest outcrops claim a prominent knoll, with a tiny ridge rising well above the tree tops. A brief scramble confirms their airy crest as a superb vantage point. Continuing on from the clearing by the crags, remain on the main track which swings up to the right. It slants to the wood top, merging with a broad access road which is followed left around to the farming hamlet and ancient settlement of Walshaw. The impressive front of the shooting lodge enjoys an enviable view down-dale.

To the right of the lodge a tiny enclosure is entered by a gate and left by a stile. Head up the yard and turn sharp right along its drive for a few yards before taking a gate on the left. From it a walled track heads away, soon becoming unenclosed and after crossing a tiny beck, rising round the top side of a larger pasture. Near the top corner a gate transfers onto the open moor, and a wide wall-side track contours round to the right beneath Shackleton Knoll. At 1215ft the highest point of the walk is reached: ubiquitous features of the view are Heptonstall church and Stoodley Pike monument.

As the environs of Crimsworth Dean are entered, the moor is vacated at a gate from where an enclosed track, Coppy Lane, descends past a ruin to a junction at Nook, another ruin. Go straight over and down the enclosed way, which quickly swings upstream to descend to Crimsworth Dean Beck, where Lumb Bridge and Lumb Hole waterfall await. This is a stunning moment as packhorse bridge and waterfalls form a delectable scene. Retrace steps briefly, but turn off the ascending main path, left through a gateway on a narrower path.

Remaining parallel with the beck, the path contours through several bracken pastures, eventually encountering a stile and the humble dwelling of Outwood before reaching a gate into the National Trust woods. From it a track rises to meet the main drive which descends unfailingly to the starting point, offering the most direct finish.

A more interesting variation ignores the gate in favour of a gap to its left, descending across the field to a stile into the woods. A path runs down to the stone arched Weet Ing Bridge which is not crossed, continuing instead on the same bank, rising a little then running along towards a gate into a field. One hundred yards before it however, rise half-right to join the main drive. This is now followed back down to Midgehole.

The falls, Lumb Hole, Crimsworth Dean

Hardcastle Crags is the name by which everyone in the district fondly knows the valley of Hebden Dale. The majority of this beautifully wooded, deep-cut dale is in the care of the National Trust, and attracts large crowds from far and wide. At the car park is a National Trust information caravan and often an ice cream van.

Turn right on the road out, crossing Horse Bridge on Crimsworth Dean Beck. The Way then takes a steep enclosed path climbing behind the toilet block. Across a track just above by a house, this superb old bridleway winds about effortlessly to gain height through the woodland of Pecket Well Clough. As height is gained the towering Wadsworth war memorial may be seen high up to the left, and can easily be visited by branching off at some old steps from where a narrow path rises steeply left. A stile gives access to the small pasture containing the striking edifice: a remarkable tribute to the lost sons of the parish. Perched above a colourful pocket of heather and gritstone outcrops it commands a glorious view, with Heptonstall church silhouetted and the environs of Hardcastle Crags outspread.

Wadsworth War Memorial, Pecket Well

The main path soon levels out to cross a stream before meeting a similar path to rise steeply onto the A6033 Keighley Road just below Pecket Well. Pecket Well is an old mill community high on the moor edge: the *Robin Hood* pub is just along to the left. **Cross straight over the main road and up a short path onto the higher Akroyd Lane.**

Turn right along the road to the second drive on the left, where the surfaced Shaw Croft Hill road rises to a handful of cottages. Here a narrow, walled path escapes to the left, rising to an open area:

either rise gradually or double back steeply up onto a firmer track, Slack House Lane. Go briefly left then strike right up an ascending, arrow-like walled track. Becoming a grassy way, at the top it emerges onto open moorland. Turn right for an extended walk along the heathery moor bottom beneath Bog Eggs Edge. At a junction by a stile in the wall, take the obvious path contouring round, just a few yards after the stile, with Bog Eggs farm and reservoir over to the right. The way unexpectedly enters enclosed ground for a spell at Old Hold.

The way runs on to absorb a drive from the house above, and on again towards the house ahead. From the gate/stile just before it, bear left up a thin path onto another track rising to a gate/stile back onto the moor, where a sustained walk ensues around Kellam Edge, under Wadsworth Moor. Initially a broad green track, it later reverts to path width. In time the way arrives beneath reclaimed quarry spoil at Cock Hill. Keep straight on the green path beneath spoil and above the start of Hebden Bridge golf course at Mount Skip. The path runs on above the clubhouse, where the upper path then slants up around the quarry spoil and along to a stile. The path then heads across a corner of Midgley Moor to a wall corner.

Continuing along the wall, taking the upper path towards the end to arrive at the prominent Churn Milk Joan. This sturdy six-footer was possibly a medieval cross, and remains to this day a well known moorland landmark. On arrival here, man's various intrusions on the moors are seen in stark contrast with the sighting of part of Ovenden Moor windfarm. **Leave on the path descending to a wall corner, and a little lower, curving left for a gentle slant across Midgley Moor.** There are long views up Cragg Vale, with the Emley Moor TV mast far beyond.

Churn Milk Joan, Midgley Moor

Another uncomplicated contour round the moor is enjoyed, being joined by a wall to curve round to a corner above an old quarry, high above Luddenden Dean. Keep left to remain on the moor edge, following the wall around to the north to reach a fence-stile giving access to a parallel farm road just below. Follow this slanting down to the surfaced end of High House Lane, where go right the few yards to the through road, Dry Carr Lane. Double back left down this, and at the third house (a very attractive one, nearest the road) go down its drive. A small gate at the corner of the yard sends the way slanting down the fieldsides below, entering a walled footway at a stile. At the bottom it emerges behind a house, Hawksclough Farm, onto the road again, now Jerusalem Lane.

Turn down this to Jerusalem Farm. This is a local authority-run education & training centre, and has toilets and a picnic site. **Double back yet again down the main track from the house on a broad, green pathway slanting down to stone arched Wade Bridge on Luddenden Brook.** It dates back to the early 19th century, having been rebuilt after flood damage. Its width shows it was meant for the passage of carts rather than mere pedestrian/equestrian use. This is a charming corner, a real place to linger as Luddenden Brook tinkles over its stony bed.

Across the bridge, take the path rising half-right through Wade Wood. This is a superb deciduous wood, comprising largely of birch, oak, beech, holly and much colourful vegetation. **At a junction double back left uphill, crossing another historic way and continue slanting up across to a corner of the wood. A grand path runs along the base of this section of the wood, with fields below and grand views over Luddenden's colourful valley. At the end of the wood the old way slants up to Upper Saltonstall, emerging beneath a house where a stile leads up onto its short drive. Head up this onto the road and turn right, briefly.** In common with neighbouring Lower Saltonstall, this hamlet was a vaccary (cattle farm) run by the Manor of Wakefield until the early 14th century. An old house on the right beneath the road features a battery of mullioned windows.

Within a few yards climb away again on a rough road. This winds up past a lone house and onto a better access road. This offers sweeping Luddenden views, from the dalehead moors right down the valley. **Go right on this, out onto the higher level Castle Carr Road, where cross straight over to a stile onto Warley Moor. An initially vague path bears off right, contouring round above the road. This grand little moorland path is aided by a series of cairns. Across a stream (the outflow from Cold Edge Dams) a more typical moorland path runs on, past a wall corner and onto a rough road.**

Turn right, and immediately after the first buildings on the left turn into the yard. Right into the 21st century this offered a surprise as it included the *Moorcock*, an isolated pub that was barely recognisable as such! **At the yard corner near the building a stile sends a path off, featuring a few flags to become enclosed beneath a small reservoir. Improving and again flagged, it runs on to a rough road by some cottages at Hoyle Bottom. Go briefly left, then take a stile on the right to cross the field to a simple plank bridge. Climb to the ladder-stile above, and from one behind it rise up the other side of the wall. At the top the path goes round the left side of Hough Gate Head Farm, and up the field to a stile/gate onto its drive. Go left on this the few yards out onto Withens Road.**

Three-quarters of a mile further up to the left stood the *Withens Hotel:* sadly this lonely moor-edge sentinel has gone the way of the *Moorcock* and is now a private house. It was built in 1862 to serve quarrymen, and was the highest pub in West Yorkshire. Above it towers the Ovenden Moor windfarm, consisting of no less than 23 wind turbines that are each 100ft high and can collectively power 7,500 homes. Try to calculate how many would be needed to supply Halifax: you would in any case need an alternative activity to rambling, because there certainly wouldn't be any room left on the moor for you and me!

Mount Zion
Methodist Church,
Upper Brockholes

Once again go left a few yards, and take a broad, part-flagged track heading away to the right. After a spell between walls it swings gently right, descending steadily into the old quarried area it once served at **Hunter Hill.** This affords a sweeping prospect over the northern Halifax suburbs, with Mixenden to the right and a golf course to the left. The name Slaughter Gap on the map is a reminder that a Civil War skirmish took place here in 1644, with the Parliamentarian forces coming off worse. **From this plateau the main path resumes the slant, leaving the quarries behind to drop more steeply out through ruined walls and grassily down onto an old walled track. Go left briefly to a little gate on the right, then cross a couple of fields to the mini-hamlet at Stod Fold.**

Passing between the buildings the access road heads away, over a brook and up to a road end. Continue up this to a junction at Lane Head, bearing right until just above another interesting hamlet, Lower Brockholes. From a stile on the left an enclosed flagged little path climbs to run on as a walled footway and along the rear of a terrace onto Per Lane at Upper Brockholes. On the left stands Mount Zion Methodist Church. Rebuilt in 1815, it features a sundial dated 1773 from the original building in which John Wesley preached. **Advance along the road to the A629 Keighley Road.** 100 yards to the left is the *Moorlands Inn,* previously the aptly named *Peat Pits.*

Cross straight over to the former *Sportsman* pub and bear right on Blind Lane, which beyond the houses becomes a green way, narrowing to an ill-drained conclusion to meet a road. With Bradshaw just along to the left, the route crosses straight over and along a short drive to a cottage, West Scausby Farm. Take the little gate into the paddock in front, and cross a field to a stile onto another drive. Go left to the yard of the hamlet (Upper West Scausby), locating the exit by an obscured gap in the jumble in front, right of the buildings. A part flagged path crosses the field towards the church, becoming a snicket on the corner to emerge between houses onto a road, Pavement Lane.

The heart of the scattered village of Bradshaw, including church and pubs is along to the left. The Way, however, goes just half a dozen yards left, and takes a stile on the right at a house drive at North Scausby Farm. Descend the fieldsides to join a rough road, School Lane. Go right, again only yards, and into another driveway and down through a private-looking gate. Note the *St John's Croft 1787* inscribed above a barn door. **Bear right to find an enclosed grassy way heading off, down behind the other buildings. Remain on it as it swings right to descend gently between fields.**

Don't go all the way down however, but when a fieldpath crosses it, take the stile on the right and head off through the fields with a massive factory ahead. In front of a new wood follow the wall outside it, becoming enclosed at the end at the start of the works. This green walled way leads on the full length of the factory to arrive at a house and small caravan site. Keep straight on out onto Holdsworth Road. Just before reaching it, easily missed on the left is the superb Holdsworth House Farm, dating from 1692 with an array of mullioned windows. **The route emerges opposite a school at Holdsworth, with the *Junction Inn* just along to the right.**

Holdsworth House Farm

Turn left down Holdsworth Road. Along a short drive on the left is Holdsworth House. Currently operating as a hotel/restaurant, this beautiful old house displays a fine frontage enhanced by a restored sunken garden, also with a gazebo in one corner. **Continue down the road to a junction, and go left on the road over the old railway cutting. Keep left on Brow Lane between works at Holmfield, with the road turning steeply uphill. Escape at the first chance up a cobbled road, Crooked Lane, which curves steeply up behind the house at Brigg Royd.** This affords fine views over north Halifax, Holmfield mills, and back over the school to Ovenden Moor windfarm.

At the top it runs on to a rough road, with the A647 Halifax-Queensbury-Bradford road just up to the left. This stage ends amid bus stops and boundary markers at 1000ft above sea level. The houses of Catherine Slack are just up to the left over the boundary with Bradford. To the south, the extensively quarried Swales Moor offers little indication of the impending loveliness of Shibden Dale.

STAGE 4

CATHERINE SLACK *to* WEST VALE

Distance: 13½ miles/21½km

Map:
1:50,000
Landranger 104 - Leeds, Bradford & Harrogate
1:25,000
Explorer 288 - Bradford & Huddersfield

➡ Having joined the A647 Halifax-Bradford road at Catherine Slack, go left just a few yards then double back right on the footway on Swales Moor Road. This is left at the first chance at cottages at Slack End. On the left a walled green bridleway winds down into woodland. Turn right at a fork, on a gentler angled path through beech woodland. This then slants down these upper reaches of Shibden Dale, across some heathery flanks. Passing through scrub keep left, a part flagged way slanting down a more open bank in this largely untainted valley.

The path runs on through a line of hollies to a stile in a gap, thence enclosed by fencing as it runs on to a stile and junction before the intriguing looking 17th century Scout Hall. Turn left here, and down through a stile an enclosed, much flagged path accompanies a tiny stream down to a stone slab footbridge on Shibden Brook. Stone steps lead up the other side to emerge onto the narrow Simm Carr Lane.

Go right a short way past a house on either side, then turn left along a nice enclosed green way. At the end take a stile on the left and along to a corner stile. A part flagged path climbs a steep bank to a stile onto an ascending enclosed way. Go right on this to Addersgate Farm and out along its drive, Addersgate Lane. This gives wide views down Shibden Dale and as far afield as Holme Moss. **The drive emerges onto a road bend, the junction of Green Lane and Paddock Road.**

Go straight ahead on the latter as far as the next bend, then leave it on a short rough way to the left. Within a few yards take a stile on the right, and climb the unkempt fieldside to a stile onto a

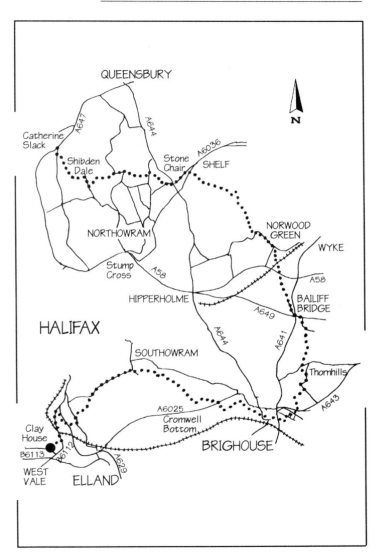

driveway. Go straight across to a contrasting densely enclosed way (Cut Lane) deep in hollies. This runs on to meet a broader bridle-track, Teal Lane, whereupon go left.

Over to the right rises the tall thin chimney of the former Northowram Hospital; the TV mast at Emley Moor is evident many miles beyond. **Teal Lane rises to run on to a bend at a lone house. Bear left up here to a track junction, and turn right to emerge onto a road. Cross straight over to a stile, and a path bears right to a farm. Keep left of the buildings, and from a stile a flagged path turns to the rear of the farmyard. Head away from the farm through a gateway and on to a clump of trees. From the stile alongside, an enclosed pathway runs on to emerge onto an urban street at Hud Hill.**

Go left on here past some curiously low cottages to the A644 at Stone Chair. Cross straight over to the attractive *Duke of York* pub. Opposite is the chair itself, inscribed *Stone Chair erected 1737 re-erected 1891*, complete with the destinations of Denholme Gate, Brighouse, Halifax and Bradford. **Head directly away along West Street (becoming Shelf Hall Lane), until just past a school the CW picks up the Brontë Way, and is shortly signed right along a snicket between houses. This emerges onto the A6036 at Shelf.**

Cross straight over and down the rough road (Bridle Stile) alongside playing fields. This descends past housing and woodland to emerge into a large field, ultimately dropping down to the farm at Dean House. En route, some good sections of paving of the original road are seen, with grooved centres worn by the passage of wheels. For much of the way there is virtually no evidence of the proximity of civilisation and industry. **At Dean House the official way differs from the logical one: neither enter the farmyard.** The easier option takes a stile on the right, and from one behind it heads past the farm environs and down the field where steps descend to a stile and plank bridge, then slants up to join the main path in the trees.

The CW proper takes a stile on the left, slanting across the field to a stile into the wooded clough. Across a simple slab bridge, 110 sturdy steps climb the other bank to join a rough access road. Turn right down this, and beyond the house a path takes over into North Wood. Remaining on high, the path savours the tree-lined environs of the beck, featuring a fine waterfall. While springtime bluebells add further character to this delectable wooded dell, the greenery of high summer all but hides the waterfall.

Just beyond this point the path leaves the wood and climbs a field to a stile at the top corner, then runs on a fieldside to become enclosed in greenery beneath a tall pylon. Coley church tower marks the skyline to the right, above the lovely wooded valley of Coley Beck beneath us. **This fine way runs on to isolated Middle Ox Heys, continuing along its drive to join Norwood Green Hill on the edge of Norwood Green. Turn left up to the brow, where a few yards right along Chapel Street is a striking clock tower.** The Ellis Memorial Clock Tower was built in 1897, and is now the classy centrepiece of a private garden. In front, here, is a delightful piece of open ground. **The through route can be rejoined by turning left past the clock tower to find snickets leading back onto the main street.**

The Way marches straight down the Village Street, passing numerous patches of ground that make 'Green' a highly appropriate name: keep on all the way to the war memorial at a junction. Numerous features of interest are passed en route. After the United Reformed Church (erected in 1882 as a Congregational Church) is St. George's church, followed by the *Old White Beare,* a white-walled inn recalling a ship that helped halt the Spanish Armada. The characterful, low roofed, multi-roomed interior owes much to its 1590 rebuilding, incorporating some timbers from the actual ship (see overleaf).

The Ellis Clock Tower, Norwood Green

On reaching the war memorial, a second pub, the *Pear Tree,* can be found to the left down Station Road. The Way goes straight on a rough road off Rookes Lane, down past a playground on the open area behind the memorial. Narrowing at the bottom, it leads **to an enviably sited cricket pitch. Alongside this the path briefly delves into a leafy enclosed way, leading to a grassy, stone-arched bridge over the Bradford-Halifax railway.** Wyke Tunnel entrance is just along to the left.

Pause also to look ahead over the Calder Valley to the Emley Moor TV mast, while on the near skyline to the left is the spire of Wyke church. **Across the bridge a path descends the field, passing through a hedge midway to meet the A58 Leeds-Halifax Road.** Over to the right, note the fading paint of a decades-old *Schweppes Table waters* advertisement where the railway line bridges the road. Over to the left stand the part-demolished remains of Wyke Viaduct, a tragically abrupt end to the sturdy arches that once carried the railway over Wyke Beck.

Cross straight over to the garden centre, and a kissing-gate into a field to its right. A thin but clearing path runs on through the field, joined by a hedge to lead pleasantly along to a stile and down to a double-slab footbridge over Wyke Beck coming in from the left. It runs on to a road end with new housing on the left. Continue straight on along Victoria Road to emerge into the centre of Bailiff Bridge. Here are shops, toilets and the *Punch Bowl* pub.

Go left, over the A641 Bradford-Brighouse road and out along the A649 rising away. Before the old rail bridge, escape to the right along Birkhouse Road. While the road bends left under a rail bridge, a rough road runs right towards a lone house, from where one can climb over the disused Bradford-Brighouse railway line back onto the road. It is in any case left at this point, turning right along an access road, Woolrow Lane. At this point we also part company with the Brontë Way, after 3½ shared miles. **The rough road leads on past a house then climbs towards the farm at Woolrow.**

The Old White Beare, Norwood Green

At the building go left a short way to a stile by a modern house, then into the field turn right to descend the fieldside. Head on through a stile and straight down through an old gateway. Overlooking a wooded little clough, the fieldside leads down to a tiny stream crossing and out onto Thornhills Beck Lane by a kennels/cattery. Turn right a short way towards the viaduct, but take a stile on the left and ascend the fieldside onto the road at Thornhills. Go right on this (Thornhills Lane) as it kinks through the hamlet and then out with fine views over Brighouse.

Part way on, a stile/gate on the right sends a path down the large field centre, meeting the former railway line again at the bottom. While folk regularly walk the old line, the Way proper turns left through the parallel wall and follows this along to emerge onto the A643 alongside the disappeared viaduct. Cross and turn down Alegar Street onto the A644 on the edge of Brighouse.

Turn right on here, left along Grove Street, then right on Mill Lane. This area is entirely industrialised, with the town centre directly in front. A short-cut runs left on a tiny street to reach Brighouse Basin on the Calder & Hebble Navigation. The designated route continues on to the *Barge* pub, then left on Wharf Street alongside Sainsbury's supermarket to a canal bridge in front of the large Millroyd Mills.

At Brighouse Basin, the presence of colourful canal boats highlights another example of the rebirth of the inland waterways network, a growing leisure industry. The Calder & Hebble Navigation was opened in 1770 to link the river Calder with the Rochdale Canal at Sowerby Bridge: at the eastern end of the basin a lock sees the waterway empty into the wide flowing river. Brighouse is the second largest community in the Calderdale district, an independent little manufacturing town that grew with the Industrial Revolution. In a refreshing turnaround from the blinkered days of railway decline, its station was re-opened in 2000.

Without crossing the bridge, turn right on the towpath to follow the Calder & Hebble Navigation through town, under road bridges and past a couple of handy, well named pubs, the *Black Swan* and the *Anchor*. Remain on this to Ganny Lock, crossing at the lock-keeper's cottage and resuming on the other bank. With the river Calder on the left, this leads to a large factory at Brookfoot Mills.

Turn right over the access bridge and along the rough North Cut out onto the A6026 Elland road. Cross straight over to find a broad path escaping on a slant up through Freeman's Wood. After a steady rise it levels out, with a fork just ahead. Keep on the more

level left branch, which then rises gently again until a sharp bend in front of two stiles. Unseen just above are the massive Cromwell Quarries, while the lake seen below at Cromwell Bottom hosts water-skiers on the site of old gravel pits.

Take the left-hand stile and almost at once a stepped descent begins, steepening and then enclosed by walls, a well-built if frustrating descent. A little over 250 not unkindly steep steps descend to behind Fort Montague Farm. By this stage we are virtually back on the valley floor, but please don't shoot the messenger! Compensation is to be found in the contrastingly genteel re-ascent.

Turn right on the walled green way, quickly entering Cromwell Wood. A super path now begins a mercurial rise, ever gently up through lovely woodland of silver birch and oak, with an older sunken way in tandem much of the way. Eventually it becomes enclosed at the top, rising still to a path crossroads. With Southowram just above, go left to curve round the very head of the clough and along to an access road. Go right just yards, then from a stile on the left rise up the fieldsides to approach a suburban scene.

From the top corner stile a fieldside path emerges onto an access road, School Lane, which runs out onto Ashday Lane alongside the old Methodist Sunday School. Turn right into Southowram at Town Gate. Just along to the right are the *Pack Horse* pub, shops and the village stocks. **Go left along West Lane, leaving the village past a massive aggregate works, and still with a footway as the road begins to descend.**

Big views look south to both Emley Moor and Holme Moss crowned by their respective TV masts, with Wainhouse Tower, much of Halifax and also Norland Moor (some 45 miles ago!) prominent ahead. **Remain on this road for a lengthy spell, until a pronounced bend right at Park Gate. Here go left on the lower of two little tracks, a few yards along to a stile/gate. Descend the fieldsides to a stile at the bottom corner. Now descend to the school playing fields corner, and pass outside them along to a stile onto Exley Lane (this final field is not waymarked in tune with the map).**

Go left on the footway to the bend at Upper Exley Farm, and take a stile on the right (earlier than the map suggests). Slant across beneath the farm building to a stile in a descending wall, which then shadow down to a stile into woods. Just below is the busy A629, also bizarrely labelled Calderdale Way! Turn right on the path in the wood, then fork left as signed (a new creation) to wind down onto the road. Cross the dual carriageway with care, and opposite, a

broad way goes left. Leave this almost at once on a path into trees, with the Calder & Hebble Navigation immediately below. Current OS maps show the route as following the A629 north-west to the A6026 junction: if Long Lees lock gate were to be open, then there is in any case no alternative but to do this.

The path runs left a short way, then double back down to Long Lees Lock. Cross with care on the lock gate upper bridge and head right, back on the towpath. Once again the river Calder is on the left, but with the noise of the road above. A nice stroll leads along to a pedestrian tunnel beneath the road bridge at the A6026/B6112 junction. Immediately through it is Salterhebble Basin, where a short branch turned off the canal to serve south Halifax. Opened in 1828, its flight of locks survive as part of a very attractive scene enhanced by numerous craft and the lock-keeper's cottage.

The Calderdale Way ignores the tunnel, and instead joins the road. Cross to the footway and turn left along the busy B6112: the Calderdale Way's least interesting half-mile comes here, with the walk's end almost within touching distance. Over the river and under a rail bridge, escape right at the first opportunity, at an old rough road opposite a sports ground. Ignoring the broad track, go straight up some wooden steps into trees and onto the old railway where the walk began. Go left through a bridle-gate/stile and the path curves round to the broader track by the wall gap behind Clay House at West Vale.

The Aisled Barn,
Clay House

A LOG OF THE WALK

Date	Place	Road	Miles stage	Miles total	Notes
	Clay House	B6112	-	-	
	Norland Moor road		2	2	
	Ripponden	A58	5¼	5¼	
	Mill Bank		6¾	6¾	
	Cragg Vale	B6138	10½	10½	
	Mankinholes		13½	13½	
	Lumbutts		½	14	
	Todmorden	A6033	2	15½	
	Centre Vale Park	A646	3¾	17¼	
	Blackshaw Head		8¾	22¼	
	Heptonstall		11½	25	
	Midgehole		½	25½	
	Pecket Well	A6033	1	26	
	Jerusalem Farm		5¾	30¾	
	Illingworth	A629	9	34	
	Holdsworth		10¾	35¾	
	Catherine Slack	A647	11½	36½	
	Stone Chair	A644	2½	39	
	Shelf	A6036	3	39½	
	Norwood Green		4¾	41¼	
	Bailiff Bridge	A649	6	42½	
	Brighouse	A644	8¼	44¾	
	Southowram		10¾	47¼	
	Clay House	B6112	13½	50	

The Country Code
• Respect the life and work of the countryside
• Protect wildlife, plants and trees
• Keep to public paths across farmland
• Safeguard water supplies
• Go carefully on country roads
• Keep dogs under control
• Guard against all risks of fire
• Fasten all gates • Leave no litter - take it with you
• Make no unnecessary noise
• Leave livestock, crops and machinery alone
• Use gates and stiles to cross fences, hedges and walls

INDEX

Principal features

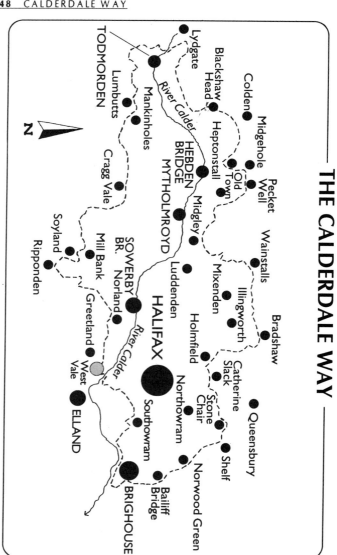

THE CALDERDALE WAY